God has victory planned for you!

Inspirational poems from God's Kingdom

Jonathan David Smith

God has victory planned for you!

ISBN: 978-1-257-10038-5

Dedication

My life and this book are dedicated to the Lord Jesus Christ. I've turned away from Him so many times, yet He's always taken me back with love and open arms. Thank You God for all that You've done, all that You're doing and all that You will do. It gives me great pleasure that You'd allow me to write these poems for You.

Email: jonathandavidministries@gmail.com

Contents

Poems

Introduction

First of all, God gets all the glory for this book. Without God, this book never, ever would have happened. Thank you Lord!!

These poems began to flow out of me within a day or so of me being obedient to something God said. I was getting out of the shower one morning and God told me to partner with a particular minister I'd been listening to for a little while. I did what I was told, and I reaped great rewards from that obedience. The anointing of God on that minister, who is now my partner, is being shared with me. Partnering with people, when led to do so by God, is an amazing thing. We are all partakers of one another's anointing when we commit to such a great task as carrying out God's will in this earth.

Some of these poems are God speaking directly to us as individuals. A few are great things for us to confess as believers. We speak them aloud in combination with God's word and it builds our faith. Faith comes by hearing the word of God, right?? We were created in God's image and He speaks things that are not, as if they already were. We are to do the same thing. We are to speak the answer and not the problem. Other poems in this book are just great inspiration from the Holy Spirit, building confidence of who we are in Christ Jesus. No longer slaves, but sons and daughters of the Most High God!!

For any of you out there that read this book of poetry and are led to put music to them, please feel free to contact me. I'd love to hear your ideas and tunes.

Confess His word out loud daily. You will begin to line up with who God created you to be. Thank God for spiritual laws that supersede natural laws!

Never forget **God loves you.**

Another day of prosperity
Has come upon me.
Yes, even more prosperity
God has given to me for free
I didn't have to buy it
Or steal or kick or fight
He gave it to me out of love
In the midst of everyone's sight.
More prosperity comes yet again my way
And I don't care what others may say
I'm not a part of the recession
It has no effect on me
I effect the economy
Evident for all to see
I merely have to comply
With whatever my Father says
Operating in His love humbly
Yes, another day of prosperity

Faith is the substance of things hoped for
The evidence of things unseen
We speak things that are not
As though they were,
As if they had already been.
We are to speak the end result
We are to speak our hearts desire.
We confess and speak it
With thankful praise
And with His Spirit
God will faithfully inspire.
He creates a vision within our soul
It is a deep passion
That goes in hand with His mission.
It is a seed that we plant,
With our words it is sown.
We thank God for the desired result
We confess and give thanks
Until it's full grown.
It manifests itself in the natural
For ourselves and even others to see
I bless you with things to enjoy greatly,
Says God, and from these
You will love to praise me.

God does things through me
No man has seen before
He created us as individuals
Because He has special things in store.
The gifts He has for me
He plans them only for my head
There are specific things in my path
That no one will get in my stead.
We have been chosen to live in these times
For a specific thing to do
God has an amazing map
For this life planned
That only you can follow through.
Do not fret because you're different
Don't be bothered because you don't fit in
A special purpose for you alone
Has been planted deep within

God loves us so much
That we cannot possibly fail
If we recite His word day and night
As high as eagles we shall sail.
Prosperity and success
Shall lead the way before us
Yes, all that we do will prosper
If we let not our obedience regress.
The Holy Spirit will teach us all things
And give us understanding of all we need.
They key is to love your neighbor as yourself
And, once again, daily to His word heed.
His love is abounding, His love is overwhelming,
His love is beyond compare.
It is that same love that we have in us
Through His son, Jesus, we have an equal share.
Height, depth, width and length
Of His love we shall understand.
For us to love one another, by faith in Jesus name
That is the superseding command.

God's army is powerful

We go marching through the land
Fully dressed in our armor
Nothing the enemy does can stand
Carrying our impermeable shield
And our quick two edged sword
We have our marching orders
Serving Yahweh, our Mighty Lord
Many of our allies have perished
From lack of knowledge on their part
We must train ourselves in scriptures
To get them within our heart
Our Commander's will
Is for us to conquer
His will is for us to win
We set our site on the Promised Land
With us at His right hand
He guides us from within

I am a cheerful giver
I'm a giver at heart
God gets my first fruits
At least a tenth I impart
Not giving under compulsion
Or doing it reluctantly
But deciding to be joyous
I am prompt to do it freely.
Offerings that I give
Are directed to where I'm fed
Blessing those that blessed me
Helps put me at peace
Knowing I planted where I was led.

I am an ambassador to the
Creator of Heaven and Earth.
The one true God, our Provider
He gives us our true worth.
Our Father lifts us above
The storms we encounter
When we lift His name on high.
He is the one who has our plan
We have been saved through our new birth.
We are the branch, He is the vine
In faithfulness, we bear fruits the same.
We stand righteous with authority
As we speak in Jesus name.
We tithe, offer, and plant seed
And God says, "Test Me in this".
We stand on this and much more,
It is our right to claim.
Then the windows of Heaven will open
And Bless us to overflow.
Jesus took the keys of death, hell, and the grave
Then He stood strong in Dunamis power
And of the devil He did make an open show.
It is His feathers of protection
Under which we abide and thrive.

(continued)

And now we are in right standing with our God
We have been made alive, alive,
Truly we are alive!!
No weapon can resist the mighty word of God
No sickness, fear, or poverty
Will we permit to survive.
We keep the Word in our eyes, mouth, and heart
To meditate on them day and night
This is how we shall have success.
We run the race to win,
And forward we shall press.
The one true God, it is His words
From which we came.
He created us in His wonderful image
It is His mold that we have been cast.
Through His blessing and Abraham's seed
We have been made the first and not the last.
I say again, I am an Ambassador
I represent the one true God.
I love Him, adore Him, and obey His word.
We lift You up and yearn for You
Lord, you have freed us of our past!

I am God's champion
As a child I had once begun
I grow every day with instruction
I am now to Him a Son
I am no longer merely a baby
I don't just live on milk
I have a zeal for the meat of God
Together we commune and talk.
I bring pleasure and joy to my Father
I serve Him with all that I am
And it is with Him that I shall walk.
I am seated in heavenly places
His perfect nature to me did He impart
I share His love and compassion
We are connected in my heart.

I do what I do
Because I love You.
I'm not concerned with the gifts
Or worried about You paying this bill
I simply choose to love you
And exercise my free will.
Even if you never answered
Another request of mine again
Love, yes love, even then
I would love you still.
I have made the decision
On record before Heaven and earth
That I love You Lord, unconditionally
I love You with all that I'm worth.
Yes I know that You will still bless me
And know that You supply all my need
But I praise and worship and honor You
I simply love you forever indeed.

I have laid the gifts before you
They're there for you to take
You just have to grab them and believe
You have to claim them to receive.
Specific gifts for you I did make
Supernatural health, abundant blessings
And grace abounding towards you.
All that you see In My word
For you is surely true.
Shake off the boundaries of this world
You have potential
Farther than the eye can see
You've been translated to the kingdom
Of my first born Son
Come get all that you can have from Me.
I've deemed the gifts to be endless
The more you receive
Means more for you to give
And for Me that's a greater witness.

I lean toward you with favor
I give you all that I am
You shall be fruitful and filled with plenty
I give you more than enough to savor
Make sure you hearken to Me
I'll give you your heart's desire
If you walk in My commands
And keep them
I assure you that your life will inspire.
All those that are around you
Many people will most assuredly stare
To try and see why you're special
They will want to know what you have
It gives you a chance to share
The wondrous joy that's in you
It's My love that's beyond compare

I no longer have a sinful nature
I have been set totally free
I have the exact same nature
Of the Almighty, One True God
Living eternally inside of me!

I praise the Lord with all my heart
I praise Him with all that I am
I praise Him with the day start
He gets praise with lifted hands
I praise the Lord as the day continues
I praise Him all the way through
I praise Him as dusk creeps on
I praise Him for blessing all that I do
I praise the Lord as the sky grows dark
I praise Him as the stars shine bright
I praise Him in advance
Of the day to come
He gets praise as I sleep through the night

I walk in God's goodness
Every day and every night
He has given His angels charge over me
And hearing His word, they take flight
His mercies are new every morning
I walk in courage and strength
I hope and expectantly wait on Him
He is always near for my comfort
His arm is never too short
My blessings pour over the rim
It is my cup that runs over
It is my dwelling that gains more and more
The Lord has blessed me with his favor.

Intimate and deep understanding
Is available to us for free
Ask for wisdom, says the Lord,
And I will give liberally.
It's no longer hidden
It's available for our eyes to see
God told us in Luke twenty-four
That we can now understand scripture
Thank God it's revealed like never before!
Abba wants a close relationship
With all of His children dear
He has so much to offer
He just wants us to draw near.
Today we make a decision
Right now we boldly declare
I commit to walking in His will
And His word will take me there

It is the blood, it is the blood
It is the blood of Jesus that has saved you.
The blood of Jesus has destroyed slavery
The blood of Jesus has set you free!
Now Say this aloud,
Every day of your life.
The blood of Jesus is sprinkled over me
The blood of Jesus has defeated the enemy
It is the blood that is my Victory!
Nothing can hold me down
Nothing can keep me bound
Victory is mine and I have no fear
The blood is on me
And NO demon can stay near
I am no longer in the pit
I am no longer a prisoner to hope
The extraordinary blood of the Lamb,
Makes me what God has spoken.
The blood of the Lamb,
The blood of the Lamb
Through the blood the bondage is BROKEN!!

It is transgressions that will ruin you
And sin that brings you to death.
All you have to do is confess them to Me.
Just repent and you will see
I throw them farther than east to west
It is I who have made you holy
I do not condemn you
I don't drag you through guilt
I bring you near with My love
And I'll wash you clean
With my Son's blood that was spilt

It is Yahweh, my God, I choose to serve
And His voice I will obey
He blesses His people beyond compare
And His word has paved the way
Your word is the perfect law of liberty
And in Your shadow I will stay
Your righteousness
Will reach across all lands
We will preach Your gospel, Yahweh
No weapon formed
Against us shall prosper
We heal the sick as our hands we lay
The demons tremble and fear
As we speak Your word
It's in Your name, Lord Jesus, we pray

Jehovah-Jirah, the Lord will provide.
Everything that has breath of life
We will lift Your Holy name on high.
You are the one that loves us
More than our minds can imagine.
You are the one true God
And our praises of Your name draw You nigh.
It is by peace and love and through Jesus'
Blood that our sins did You atone
You have given us access
To boldly approach the throne.
We, without You, were lost and dead
But Your Grace, to us, did You provide.
We can swear by no higher,
To the King of heaven and earth,
That we will obey Your word
While we lift our hands to the sky.
We are now joint heirs with Jesus
Full partners and covenant bound.
All things have been put under our feet
And even though the devil may try
We are more than conquerors
In Jesus Christ
And our spirit, it no longer will die.

The blood has drawn me near
The blood has made me rich
The blood has made me whole
The blood has saved my soul
The blood makes new songs to flow
The blood has made me white as snow
The blood has made me guilt free
I have access to the throne
For all eternity

Jesus is your peace
The Holy Ghost is your comfort
Glory to God in the Highest
Of earth, I gave man a lease.
Over this, you will dominate,
Rule, reign, and multiply.
For this you are created,
You are the apple of My eye.
For 6,000 years
I have given you control.
Yes, for this you were created
You will step into My role.
Although Adam had sinned
And allowed death, fear, and lack;
Jesus, the head of the church,
Has won all the authority back.
You are not of this world,
You are named of God Himself.
Meditate on Me, renew your mind
And know that you are
Of Heaven's commonwealth.
You are kings, priests, and prophets
And abundant grace and favor on you overtake.
Walk in My ways and obey My word
Of you a peculiar people I did make.
(continued)

My blessing is upon you
And I say it makes you rich.
I watch over My word so it does as I've said
It is absolutely, positively true.
And don't you forget the biggest thing of all
Is that I unconditionally love you.

Loving-kindness from You is endless
Your mercy abundantly great
Love for us is everlasting
On You alone, we expectantly wait.
You flood us with heaping blessings
For our foundation You're our solid rock
The creator of the depths of the oceans
You're our Shepherd
And we are Your flock.
You prepare a great feast before the eyes
Of all our sworn enemies
They look upon us with despise
Yet You have rescued us with honor
In You, there is no compromise.
There is no wrong in You Lord
Your kingdom is continually upright
We've been rescued from the darkness
With Your grace,
You've brought us to light.

My eyes are wide open
My heart is eager to hear
My lips speak your scriptures
And I know You will draw near
My passion is for You, Lord
My zeal is burning white hot
My spirit cries for Abba, my Daddy
I am pursuing all that You've got.
I have a direct connection to You
I need You for all that You are
Nothing else in this world satisfies me
Like You, my bright morning star
My want for You is growing deep
Your presence fills my every void
My love for you is multiplied daily
It is You that makes me overjoyed

My flesh is not in charge of me
I don't allow it to run freely
I keep it in line, according to the word
I speak to my body daily.
I put no trust in physical appearance
I put no confidence in the flesh
My trust is in the Spirit
And not in worldly occurrence.
God has made me a Spirit
To temporarily live in this body
We are to keep it as a temple
Through discipline we keep it holy.
I'm not saying that slips don't happen
That falls will not occur
But I put on the Divine nature
My trust in God is what makes me sure.

My leaves don't wither
And my branches are strong
I bear much fruit
For my roots are long.
I'm planted by a river
Buried deep in the word
I'm not affected by drought
It's God's voice that I've heard.
Surely storms will come
And try to topple me over
By my seed is buried firmly
By the word of His power.
I have not a care
For I have been made just
I yield abundant harvest
Because in the Lord I trust

My love is endless and perfect
My love is patient and pure
Always abounding towards you
There is no emptiness it cannot cure
Things of this world are unstable
Even my own children can let you down
But you have My word I'll never fail you
And of that you can eternally be sure.

Love Forever,
God

Peace be still
Is what Jesus said to the storm
Peace be still
And it immediately took new form.
There was no fear in Him
He had already said, Let us cross
The sudden circumstance couldn't prevail
Our Savior, through words, was the boss.
We have been created
In the same exact way
We are to say what we mean
And mean what we say.
When a storm arises against us
And they shall surely come
We rebuke the coming onslaught
Standing faithfully on what's been done.
We are not moved by tribulation
Any sudden circumstance
By faith we see shoreline
Trusting in Him we take our stance.
Satan you cannot stop me
I'm a child of the living God
I rebuke your attack, in Jesus name
Get out of the way, you're just a fraud.

(No sickness can cling)
Sickness, viruses
Plagues, disease
And whatever else
The devil may bring
Can't survive in our body
We give them no place to cling.
By Jesus' stripes
We were totally healed
We've been sprinkled by His blood
Nothing can penetrate that shield
We are no longer under the law
God's will is perfect health
We are to confess healing scriptures
By faith we do it our self.
Don't misunderstand, I'm not saying
That God isn't involved
But we are to agree with His word
And we have authority
To get the problem solved.
Our faith comes by hearing
So read the scriptures aloud
You'll become an over comer
You'll make your Heavenly Father proud

Plant the seed of gladness
Plant the seed of joy
Give it to others who are in need
The fruits of the spirit you should employ
People need My kindness
My patience and My peace
They have to have it coming through you
You are my wonderful mouthpiece.
Speak to strangers with compassion
And to those you know with love
I want them to know who I truly am
You have this responsibility from above.

(Please sit and think about this for a moment)

Praise you Jesus

Praise the Lord!
Your word is mighty,
Like a two-edged sword.
We cannot be defeated,
We are born of Abraham’s seed.
We have been bought with a price
Our God shall meet our every need.
His grace abounds to us,
It overtakes us like a flood.
All our sins are washed away,
We are saved by Christ’s precious blood.
Old things have passed away
And now we think on things above
He has made us more than conquerors
And nothing can separate us from His love.

Thank You so much
For all that You do
You protect me from danger
And keep me close to You
Thank you so much
For all that You are
My Savior, My Comforter
Always near, never far
Thank you so much
For all that You've said
You've laid out my path
Graciously anointed my head
Thank You so much
For the price that You paid
You sacrificed Yourself
On the alter you were laid
Thank You so much
For making me who I am
I'm a citizen of Heaven
Joint heir with the Lamb

The blood of My Son Jesus
It has been poured on your head.
Old things have passed away
For your sins He died in your stead.
You were purchased for a purpose
A great cost was your life.
Blood bought and created new
This ultimate plan I made for you.
You are no longer under the curse
The veil has been torn
Jesus was my only son
But now, great multitudes have been born!
Do not fear and do not worry
To Me that is a sin.
Cast all your cares on Me
I'll do the caring for you.
Focus on Me, obey My word,
And remember
It's you that has the tools to win.

The Holy Spirit stirs
In the depths of my soul
It is explosive, dynamite power
But gentle and under control.
It is a fiery consuming zeal
A great passion from within
It is our comforter that is moved by faith
And not by how we feel.
It is our bright and shining light
That utters groaning and tongues
It speaks only what it hears
At times it's an intercessory fight.
No demon and no devil
Can stop the words that flow
God Himself watches over the words
And the angels, to carry them out, they go.
The Spirit speaks God's perfect will
It brings forth His true desire
If we submit and let Him work
He will only bring us higher

The outpouring of My Spirit
Has drawn very near
For those intimate with Me
That has already been made clear
You know the Holy Spirit is saying
It is time, the harvest is here.
For those of you pretending
And only playing church
It's time to get your head on straight
And come down from your high perch.
The demons know their time is short
I want you safe and secure
If your trust isn't fully in Me
You open yourself to danger
And the drought will come for sure.
However, if you repent
And allow Me to draw near
Regardless of circumstance
You will flourish
And in your camp there shall be no fear.

The thoughts come in
But I don't give them root
They try to grab hold
But I shake them
And give them the boot.
They're grabby and possessive
Yet I stand on what I've been told
I refuse to give in
I will take charge and be bold.
God has said in His word
My thoughts are not your thoughts
My ways are not your ways
Think of things above
I'll get you through the days.
Then I say out loud with my mouth
Thoughts, I give you no place
I have the mind of Christ
You're not welcome, leave no trace.
My words are powerful and quick
Life and death are within the tongue
I have dominion over my life
Things are not just up to chance
I refuse to let circumstance dictate.
(Continued)

I say what God says
About me in His word
With my words I shall create
The environment of God's will around me
With confidence I step to the plate.
I absolutely positively refuse
To let the darkness penetrate me
And with God's word I will not lose.

Through all the junk I persevere
Through tribulation I press through
No matter what comes my way
I keep my focus on You.
However difficult the journey may seem
As it tries to stay in my face
I will accomplish what God has planned
I run to win this race.
Winning isn't everything
Some people justify and say
But what excuse will they have
When before God on judgment day?
I will press through, I will run
I will not quit with falter
This tenacity God has given us
So we are justified, standing at the altar.
God loves you so much
You've been born with incorruptible seed
Keep pushing through to finish
He has met our every need.

Upon me is anointing
It is abundantly clear.
I surrender my all
I shall not have any fear.
I ask You to steer me through life
Through all You've predestined for me.
It was all planned before
The foundation of the world
And now it's been gloriously unfurled.
I dare not live in denial
Thinking I can't believe all this is true
Only will I say what You've said
I'm trusting fully in only You.
The abundant prosperity You've given me
Is scoffed at by some
But I don't care about what they say
I say let all the blessings come!!

We are hewn from the Rock
And dug from the quarry
We are imputed with right standing
And partakers of His glory.
Only one sacrifice was needed
For the remission of all sin
We are to put on the new man
A God like new creation from within.
Drawn out of the darkness
Into the Kingdom of His Son
Reconciled by the blood
Our journey has just begun.
Spiritual death, poverty, and lack
Was all that we had before
But the Lambs blood cancelled it all
And He will remember our sin no more

We are to expect God to move every day
We are to seek His face
And we shall continually pray
He is moved by faith
And it is that alone
We are joint heirs with His son
We are to boldly approach the throne.
When we step towards Him
Being doers of His word
He will move mountains and seas
Because we took actions on what we heard

We celebrate Your name Lord
We lift You up with our praise Lord
We clap our hands with Joy
We raise our arms to the sky
Jesus You have redeemed us
Through Your blood
We have been washed
You took our sins away
We praise you every day
You've shined Your light upon us
Set a pathway before us
The victory is ours
We live our lives as Yours
We sing our praises to You God
Thank you for all that You've done
We declare that we've won
Through your firstborn Son

We give You glory
And cry out Your Name
To a dying world
It's You we boldly proclaim
You are our shield
Our immovable rock
You always stay the same
Enter our midst with your sweet presence
Come and fill this place
We longingly seek Your face

We live behind great walls
Of fortified defense
No weapon can get through
Nothing made will advance
We stand on our Rock
And our foundation is settled.
In this world of darkness
We are entrenched and embattled
We wrestle not with flesh and blood
But against satan and principalities
Jehovah Shammah is my shield
The demons are quaking at the knees.
We are not only on the defensive
But an unprecedented offensive move
We go on the attack
And take action for God to prove
That in the name of Jesus
And through His reconciling blood
By the word of our testimony
We have overtaken that old serpent
Like an all encompassing flood!

You are My creation
You are My joy
Don't let them tell you you're worthless
You are not a lowly worm
That's a lie! It's satan's ploy
You've been made a royal priesthood
You are the righteousness of Me
Do not give into that bondage
You have been set forever free!
I gave you the blessing
I gave you My grace
Don't confess what the world says
It is on you that I have shined My face.
The only way you can fail
Is if you totally quit
Pull up your boot straps
Brush off the dust
And keep your eyes on Me.
Be strong and of good courage
Be sober and vigilant too
I have given you all you need
Victory is yours through and through

Your blessing is upon Your people
It's a torrential downpour on our lands
We prosper in all that we do
You've blessed the works of our hands
We are excited to please You Lord
We jump to obey Your commands
Your covenant stays with us all our days
The blessings outnumber
All the grains of sand

Scripture references:

Another day of prosperity- Deut. 8:18, Deut. 28:1-12, Psalm 1:1-3, Psalm 34:8-10, II Corinthians 9:6-11, III John 1:2

Faith is the substance of things hoped for- Hebrews 11:1-16, Matthew 17:20, Romans 4:17, Hebrews 10:23, Mark 11:23-24, 1 Timothy 6:17

God does things through me-1 Corinthians 12:12-31, Psalm 139:13-16, Romans 8:31

God loves us so much- John 3:16, John 14:16, John 15:13-17, Luke 24:45, Hebrews 13:8, Ephesians 3:16-21, Psalm 36:5-10 1 John 4:9-12, Romans 8:35-39, John 14:26

God's army is powerful-Psalm 144:1, Hosea 4:6, Ephesians 6:10-18, Hebrews 4:12, Luke 10:19-20, Matthew 28: 18-20, Isaiah 54:17, Romans 8:31

I am a cheerful giver-2 Corinthians 9:6-11, Malachi 3:10-12, Luke 6:38

I am an ambassador-Hebrews 6:19-20, Philippians 4:19, Matthew 6:31-32, Luke 12:7, 2 Corinthians 9:8, John 15:5, 2 Corinthians 5:21, Joshua 1:3-9, Genesis 1:27, Philippians 3:12-20, Galatians 3:29, Isaiah 54:17, Revelation 1:18, Hebrews 10:22

I am God's champion-Ephesians 2:6, 1 John 3:2, Romans 8:15, 2 Peter 1:4, Hebrews 13:6, Galatians 5:22-23,

I do what I do-Mark 12:30-34, Deuteronomy 10:12

I have laid the gifts before you-Colossians 1:13-14, Ephesians 3:20-21, James 1:17, Romans 11:29, Acts 8:18-20

I lean towards you with favor-Ephesians 2:7, Malachi 3:12, Job 10:12, Psalm 5:12, Psalm 89:17, Proverbs 3:10

I no longer have a sinful nature-Hebrews 10:10, 12-14, 22, 2 Peter 1:4

I praise the Lord with all my heart-Psalm 103, Psalm 1

I walk in God's goodness-Psalm 91:11, Luke 4:10, Psalm 23, Isaiah 59:1, Micah 6:8
Intimate and deep understanding-Ephesians 1:17, 1 Corinthians 2:1-16, Luke 24:45, James 1:5, Psalm 111:10
It is the blood-Hebrews 9:13-15, Hebrews 10:12, 14, 17, 19, 22, Romans 5:9-11, Colossians 3:1-4, Isaiah 43:25, 1 John 1:7, Revelation 12:11
It is transgressions that will ruin you-Romans 6:23, Hebrews 10:22, 1 John 1:7-9, Psalm 103:11-12, Isaiah 43:25, Hebrews 8:12
It is Yahweh-Joshua 24:24, James 1:25, Isaiah 54:17, Matthew 10:8, Psalm 91:1
Jehovah-Psalm 150:6, Psalm 22:3, Hebrews 22:19, Ephesians 3:6, 1 Corinthians 15:27, Romans 8:37-39, 1 John 5:11
Jesus' blood- Romans 5:10, 2 Corinthians 5:18, Romans 10:10, Romans 9:14, Psalm 33:3, Psalm 96:1
Jesus is our peace-Genesis 1:26-30, Zechariah 2:8, Colossians 2:15, Malachi 3:17, Titus 2:14, Psalm 3:8, Proverbs 10:22, John 17:14, Isaiah 55:11
Loving-Kindness from You is endless-Psalm 36:7, Jeremiah 31:3, Psalm 23, Psalm 31:3, Psalm 62:2, Psalm 5:3
My eyes are wide open-Revelation 22:16, John 15:4, Psalm 69:9, Psalm 119:11, Mark 12:30
My flesh is not in charge of me-Romans 12:2, Philippians 3:3, Romans 9:20, Galatians 5:1-25,
My leaves don't wither-Jeremiah 17:7-8, Psalm 1:1-3, John 16:33
My love is endless and perfect-1 Corinthians 13:4-8, Lamentations 3:22, Psalm 28:28, John 3:16
Peace, be still-Mark 4:35-41, Genesis 1:26-27, Mark 11:23, Luke 17:6, John 16:33, Luke 10:19, Matthew 28:18-20

No sickness can cling-1 Peter 2:24, Isaiah 54:17, Psalm 91:5-10, Deuteronomy 28:15-61, Galatians 3:13, Romans 10:17, Joshua 1:8, 1 John 4:4

Plant the seed of gladness-Mark 12:32-33, Ephesians 2:10, Galatians 5:22-23, Luke 6:31, Luke 6:38, Colossians 3:12-14

Praise you Jesus-1 Corinthians 6:20, 1 Corinthians 7:23, Acts 20:28, 2 Corinthians 5:17, Hebrews 10:22, 1 John 1:7, Galatians 3:29, 2 Corinthians 1:3-4, Hebrews 4:12

Thank You so much-Psalm 91, Romans 8:17, Philippians 3:20, Ephesians 2:19, Deuteronomy 31:5, 8, Joshua 1:5-6, John 1:9

The blood of My Son Jesus-Hebrews 10:22, Hebrews 10:19, 1 John 1:7, Galatians 3:13, 1 Peter 5:7-8, Psalm 55:22, Hebrews 9:14, Ephesians 6:10-18, 2 Corinthians 5:17, Psalm 5:11-12, Colossians 1:14-18, Matthew 27:51

The Holy Spirit stirs-Matthew 3:11, Acts 2:3-4, 17-18, John 2:7, Romans 8:26, Psalm 104:4, Psalm 103:20, John 14:26, Hebrews 2:4 2 Timothy 1:7

The outpouring of My spirit- Isaiah 44:3, Joel 2:28, John 14:15-17, John 14:25-27, Acts 1:8, Hebrews 10:22, Ezekiel 36:25-27, Matthew 24:4-31, Isaiah 9:2

The thoughts come in-Isaiah 55:8-9, 2 Corinthians 10:4-5, Romans 12:2, Psalm 119:15-16, Joshua 1:3-9, 1 Corinthians 2:16, Proverbs 18:21, James 3:1-12, Colossians 3:1-2, Acts 4:29, Colossians 1:13, Acts 26:18, John 1:5, Isaiah 9:2

Through all the junk I persevere- John 17:4, Proverbs 3:5-6, John 16:33, Romans 8:31-39, Matthew 7:7, Philippians 4:13, Philippians 3:14, 1 Peter 1:22-23, Psalm 34:6-10, Habakkuk 2:4

Upon me is anointing-Psalm 37:23-24, Jeremiah 1:5, Matthew 25:34, John 15:16, Deuteronomy 28:1-14, James 1:17-18, 1 Peter 2:9-10

We are hewn from the Rock-Isaiah 51:1, 1 Peter 1:3-4, Hebrews 10:10, Hebrews 10:19, Ephesians 2:1-22, Colossians 1:13, Revelation 12:11

We are to expect God to move every day-Hebrews 11:6, Hebrews 10:19, James 1:22, Matthew 6:33, Luke 12:31, Romans 8:17, Psalm 5:3, 1 Chronicles 16:11, Exodus 14:21-29

We celebrate Your name Lord-Isaiah 60:1, Hebrews 10:22, Psalm 47:1-2, Psalm 134:1-3, Proverbs 12:28, 1 Peter 1:2, 1 John 5:4, Psalm 47:6-7

We give You glory-Revelations 14:7, Joshua 7:19, Isaiah 42:12, Matthew 18:20, 1 Corinthians 10:4, 2 Samuel 22:47, Exodus 15:2

We live behind great walls-Psalm 91, Isaiah 54:16-17, Psalm 23, Deuteronomy 32:30-31, 2 Samuel 22:44-51

You are My creation-Genesis 1:26-30, 1 Peter 2:9, 1 Chronicles 28:20, Joshua 1:5-9, Joshua 10:25, 1 Thessalonians 5:6, 1 Peter 4:7, Philippians 4:13, John 1:16, Psalm 3:8, Matthew 10:14, Ephesians 6:15

Your blessing is upon Your people-Psalm 3:8, Proverbs 10:22, Deuteronomy 2:7, Deuteronomy 28:1-14, Hebrews 9:15, 3 John 1:2

JEHOVAH--YAHWEH.....Genesis 2:4

A reference to God's divine salvation.

JEHOVAH-SHAMMAH.......Ezekiel 48:35

"The Lord who is present"

JEHOVAH-RAPHA.........Exodus 15:26

"The Lord our healer"

JEHOVAH-NISSI.........Exodus 17:15

"The Lord our banner"

www.ingramcontent.com/pod-product-compliance
Ingram Content Group UK Ltd.
Pitfield, Milton Keynes, MK11 3LW, UK
UKHW020233250726
13967UKWH00001B/345